What Is Technology?

Cynthia O'Brien

CRABTREE
PUBLISHING COMPANY
WWW.CRABTREEBOOKS.COM

Title-Specific Learning Objectives:

Readers will:
- Define a technology as a tool that helps us do work, and makes life easier, safer, and more fun.
- Identify and explain examples of technologies.
- Ask and answer questions about technologies, and identify the main ideas in the text.

High-frequency words (grade one) a, all, and, are, be, do, if, is, it, make, of, that, the, us	Academic vocabulary build, equipment, protect, smoke detector, tablet, technology, temperature, thermometer

Before, During, and After Reading Prompts:

Activate Prior Knowledge and Make Predictions:

Have children read the title and look at the image on the title page. Create a KWL chart and fill in the "Know" and "Want to Know" sections together. Ask:

- What do you know about technology?
- Do you know the definition of technology?
- What are some examples of technologies?
- What do you want to know about technology?

During Reading:

After reading pages 4 and 5, ask children:

- Does the information on these pages help answer the question, "What is technology?"
- What words help you find the answer?
- Can you define technology in your own words?

After Reading:

Create a child-friendly definition of technology and put it on an anchor chart. Make a chart of technologies and their purposes. On one side of the chart, list the technologies that are mentioned in this book. On the other side, write down the purpose of the technology. For example: Oven—Makes cooking easier. Have children create their own charts with 5-8 examples of technologies in the classroom or at home.

Author: Cynthia O'Brien

Series Development: Reagan Miller

Editor: Janine Deschenes

Proofreader: Melissa Boyce

STEAM Notes for Educators: Janine Deschenes

Guided Reading Leveling: Publishing Solutions Group

Cover, Interior Design, and Prepress: Samara Parent

Photo research: Cynthia O'Brien and Samara Parent

Production coordinator: Katherine Berti

Photographs:
iStock: kali9: p. 6 (right); ranckreporter: p. 11 (bottom); sturti: p. 13; Solovyova: p. 15; Steve Debenport: p. 19 (bottom); bukharova: p. 20
All other photographs by Shutterstock

Library and Archives Canada Cataloguing in Publication

O'Brien, Cynthia (Cynthia J.), author
    What is technology? / Cynthia O'Brien.

(Full STEAM ahead!)
Includes index.
Issued in print and electronic formats.
ISBN 978-0-7787-6204-1 (hardcover).--
ISBN 978-0-7787-6249-2 (softcover).--
ISBN 978-1-4271-2260-5 (HTML)

    1. Technology--Juvenile literature. 2. Technology--Social aspects--Juvenile literature. I. Title.

T48.O28 2019   j600   C2018-906165-0
                                        C2018-906166-9

Library of Congress Cataloging-in-Publication Data

Names: O'Brien, Cynthia, author.
Title: What is technology? / Cynthia O'Brien.
Description: New York, New York : Crabtree Publishing Company, 2019.
   | Series: Full STEAM Ahead! | Includes index.
Identifiers: LCCN 2018056590 (print) | LCCN 2018059400 (ebook) |
   ISBN 9781427122605 (Electronic) |
   ISBN 9780778762041 (hardcover : alk. paper) |
   ISBN 9780778762492 (pbk. : alk. paper)
Subjects: LCSH: Technology--Juvenile literature. |
   Tools--Juvenile literature.
Classification: LCC T48 (ebook) | LCC T48 .O2734 2019 (print) |
   DDC 600--dc23
LC record available at https://lccn.loc.gov/2018056590

Printed in the U.S.A./042019/CG20190215

Table of Contents

Crabtree Publishing Company

www.crabtreebooks.com   1-800-387-7650

Published in Canada
Crabtree Publishing
616 Welland Ave.
St. Catharines, Ontario
L2M 5V6

Published in the United States
Crabtree Publishing
PMB 59051
350 Fifth Avenue, 59th Floor
New York, New York 10118

Published in the United Kingdom
Crabtree Publishing
Maritime House
Basin Road North, Hove
BN41 1WR

Published in Australia
Crabtree Publishing
Unit 3 – 5 Currumbin Court
Capalaba
QLD 4157

What is Technology?

Technology is the tools that help us do work. There are many kinds of technology all around us. It helps make life easier, safer, and more fun.

A soccer ball is a technology that makes life more fun! Soccer shoes make it easier to run and kick the ball.

tablet

A tablet is a technology. It shows us pictures, videos, and words. It makes learning easier and more fun.

At School

We use technology at school to help make learning easier.

pencil

crayon

A pencil is a technology that makes it easier to write.

A crayon is a technology that makes it easier to draw colorful pictures.

chair

desk

Desks and chairs are technologies that make learning easier.
A desk gives us a place to do work. A chair gives us a place to sit.

Helping to Build

People **build** the things they need.
They build houses. They build **furniture**.
They use technology to make building easier.

saw

A saw is a technology that makes it easier to cut wood.

hammer

nail

A hammer makes it easier to put nails into wood.
A nail is a technology too. It holds the pieces of wood together.

Around the House

Technologies can help make life easier and safer at home. What technologies do you use at home?

vacuum cleaner

A vacuum cleaner picks up dirt. It helps make cleaning easier.

railing

Railings make using stairs safer. People hold them so they do not fall.

oven

An oven is a technology that makes cooking food easier.

Staying Safe

Many technologies make life safer.
They can **protect** us from being hurt.
They can warn us if there is danger.

helmet

A helmet helps you stay safe when you ride a bike or scooter.
It protects your head if you fall.

smoke
detector

A smoke detector helps keep us safe. It warns us that there might be a fire.

In the Car

The technologies in cars make life safer. All people wear seat belts in cars. Small children sit in car seats.

car seat

seat belt

A seat belt holds a person safely in their seat.
A car seat fits small children. It holds them safely in their seat too.

mirrors

Mirrors are technologies that can keep us safe. They help drivers see what is behind them.

On the Road

Technology helps drivers stay safe on the road. **Traffic** lights make driving safer.

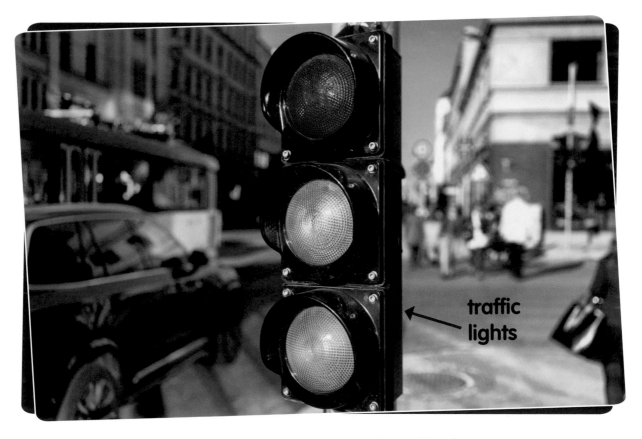

traffic lights

A green light tells drivers to go. A red light tells drivers to stop. A yellow light tells drivers to slow down.

A crosswalk is a technology that keeps us safe. It tells us where to safely cross a road.

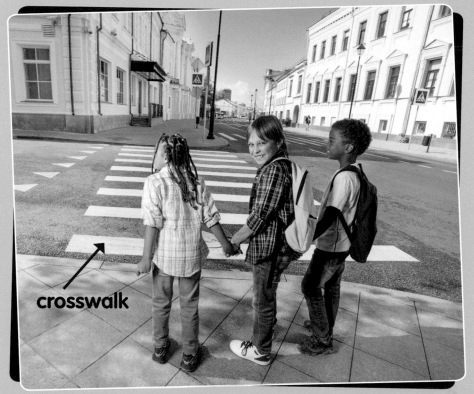

crosswalk

street sign

Technology can help make driving easier. Street signs help drivers find their way.

Staying Healthy

Technologies can help keep us **healthy**. They can help us feel better when we are sick.

bandage

A bandage covers a scratch. This helps the scratch to **heal**.

A thermometer takes your **temperature**. If you are too warm, you might be sick.

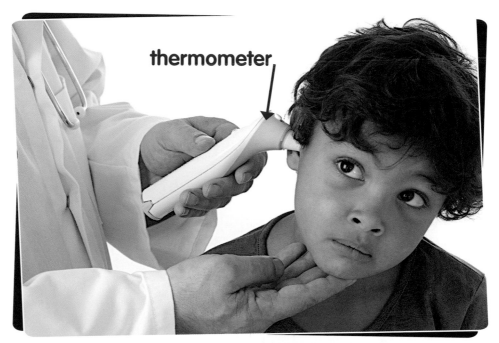

thermometer

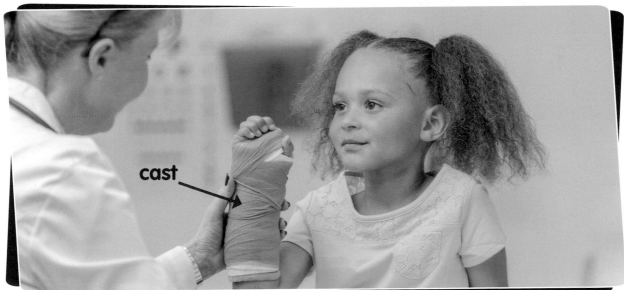

cast

A cast helps broken bones to heal.

Time to Play

Many technologies make life more fun! Can you think of other things that make your life more fun?

roller coaster

A roller coaster is a technology that makes life more fun!

Do video games make your life more fun?

Playground **equipment** makes life more fun! It helps you climb, jump, slide, and swing!

Words to Know

build [bild] verb To make by putting together parts

equipment [ih-KWIP-muhnt] noun Things used for a certain purpose

furniture [FUR-ni-cher] noun Objects in a room such as a chair, table, or bed

heal [heel] verb To fix or get better

healthy [HEL-thee] adjective Not sick or hurt

protect [pruh-TEKT] verb To keep from being hurt

temperature [TEM-per-uh-cher] noun How hot or cold something is

traffic [TRA-fik] noun All the cars, trucks, and other vehicles driving along a road

A noun is a person, place, or thing.

A verb is an action word that tells you what someone or something does.

An adjective is a word that tells you what something is like.

Index

About the Author

Cynthia O'Brien has written many books for young readers. It is fun to help make a technology like a book! Books can be full of stories. They also teach you about the world around you, including other technologies.

To explore and learn more, enter the code at the Crabtree Plus website below.

www.crabtreeplus.com/fullsteamahead

Your code is:
fsa20

STEAM Notes for Educators

Full STEAM Ahead is a literacy series that helps readers build vocabulary, fluency, and comprehension while learning about big ideas in STEAM subjects. *What is Technology?* uses repeated text and examples to help readers answer questions about technology and identify the main ideas in the text. The STEAM activity below helps readers extend the ideas in the book to build their skills in technology, engineering, and language arts.

My Technology Idea

Children will be able to:
- Define technology as the tools that help us do work, and give examples of technology that make life easier, safer, and more fun.
- Create a plan for a technology that can be used in their community.

Materials
- My Technology Idea Planning Sheet
- My Technology Idea
- Whiteboard and markers

Guiding Prompts
After reading *What is Technology?*, ask children:
- What is technology? Can you give a definition of technology in your own words?
- How can technology make learning easier? How can it make home life safer? How can it make your community more fun?

Activity Prompts
Explain to children that engineers are the people who design technologies. They use science, math, and creative thinking to design technologies that solve problems and meet needs. The technologies they design make life easier, safer, and more fun.

Tell children that they will act like engineers and create an idea for their own technology!

Each new technology idea comes from a problem or a need. Brainstorm some problems and needs. Write down the ideas on the whiteboard for children to use as jumping-off points.

Hand each child the My Technology Idea Planning Sheet. Review criteria for technology:
- Must solve a problem or meet a need.
- Must make life easier, safer, or more fun.

When children are finished planning, they can create a good copy on the My Technology Idea. They need to draw a picture and describe the problem it solves or need it meets. They also need to identify if it makes life easier, safer, or more fun. Then, have children present their technology ideas.

Extensions
- Have children create an advertisement that convinces others to use the new technology.
- Introduce children to the engineering design process. Have them follow the process to create a finished version of their technology.

To view and download the worksheets, visit **www.crabtreebooks.com/resources/printables** or **www.crabtreeplus.com/fullsteamahead** and enter the code **fsa20**.